THE
Bon Appétit
KITCHEN
COLLECTION

Gifts from your Kitchen

**The Knapp Press
Publishers**

Los Angeles

D0042765

Bon Appétit® is a registered trademark of
Bon Appétit Publishing Corp.
Used with permission.

Published by The Knapp Press
5900 Wilshire Boulevard, Los Angeles,
California 90036

Library of Congress Cataloging in Publication
Data
Main entry under title:

Gifts from your kitchen.

(The Bon appétit kitchen collection)
Includes index.
1. Cookery. 2. Gifts. I. Series.
TX652.G54   1983   641.5   83-13621
ISBN 0-89535-122-6

Printed and bound in the United States of
America

On the Cover: *Windmill Cookies, Brown
Sugar Pecan Brownies, Christmas Fruitcake*

Photograph by Alan Krosnick

Contents

Cheeses, Spreads and Nuts

Walnut and Port Cheese

Makes about 1 cup

- 1 cup cream cheese
- 2 tablespoons powdered sugar
- 2 tablespoons Port
  Chopped walnuts

Blend together cheese and sugar. Using a table knife, swirl Port through cheese, making streaks but not blending in completely. Form into ball. Wrap and chill at least 4 hours. Before serving, press walnuts firmly into top and sides of cheese.

Rumanian Cheese

Serve with thinly sliced dark pumpernickel.

Makes 5 cups

- 2 cups feta cheese
- 2 cups (4 sticks) unsalted butter
- 1 cup cream cheese

Mix in blender or processor. Transfer to crock and refrigerate until using.

Chili Cheese Balls

Delicious with dried figs and apricots.

Makes 3½ to 4 dozen

- 3 cups grated Monterey Jack cheese
- 1 cup grated Fontina cheese
- 1 3-ounce package cream cheese, room temperature
- 4 teaspoons prepared mustard
- 1 teaspoon Worcestershire sauce
- ½ teaspoon garlic powder
- 4 teaspoons chili powder

Combine first 6 ingredients with 2 teaspoons chili powder and shape into bite-size balls. Sprinkle remaining chili powder in large bowl, add cheese balls and toss gently to coat. Chill.

Trieste Cheese Spread

Try this Italian variation of Liptauer. Use on rounds of black pumpernickel accompanied by crisp radish roses. Recipe may be doubled.

Makes about 3½ cups

- 1 1½-inch piece leek, white part only
- ½ pound Gorgonzola cheese, room temperature
- 6 ounces cream cheese, room temperature
- ½ cup (1 stick) unsalted butter, room temperature
- 2 tablespoons grated onion
- 1 tablespoon caraway seed
- 1 flat anchovy, drained and chopped

½ tablespoon capers, drained

¼ teaspoon prepared mustard

¼ teaspoon paprika

Half and half (optional)

Cook leek in water until tender; drain, mash and set aside.

Combine Gorgonzola, cream cheese and butter in large bowl and blend with wooden spoon or electric mixer, or place in food processor and mix well. Add reserved leek. Continuing to stir or blend, add remaining ingredients except half and half. If mixture seems too thick, thin with half and half until desired consistency. Spoon into crock and chill several hours.

Spread may be refrigerated up to 1 week.

Homemade Cottage Cheese

Cottage cheese fanciers will find it hard to match this creamy homemade variety.

Makes about 3 cups

> 1 gallon nonfat milk
> ½ junket rennet tablet
> ¼ cup cold water
> ¼ cup cultured buttermilk
>
> Salt (optional)
> ⅓ cup 5% butterfat milk or whipping cream (optional)

Heat nonfat milk in top of a large double boiler (or improvise one with two pots) to 72°F. While milk is heating, crush rennet tablet in the water. Add rennet solution and buttermilk to the warm milk and stir well.

Remove milk from the water bath, cover and let stand in a warm place for 12 to 18 hours, or until a firm curd is formed. (In order to maintain a temperature of 72°F to 80°F, place the pan of milk in a kettle of warm water, replacing when needed, or set on heating pad. A gas oven with pilot light or electric oven with bulb on also works.)

When the curd has the consistency of pudding, cut it with a long knife or a curd cutter across and at an angle in ½-inch cubes. Return inner pan containing milk to the double boiler and heat until curd reaches 110°F. Keep curd at this temperature 15 to 20 minutes, stirring at 5-minute intervals to heat curd uniformly.

When curd is firm, line a colander with several thicknesses of rinsed cheesecloth and pour in the curd. Drain. When the liquid (the whey) has drained 5 to 10 minutes, gather the cheesecloth together and lift the curd from the colander. Immerse in a pan of ice water, working gently with your hands, until thoroughly chilled, about 5 minutes. Lift curd from colander and gently squeeze out liquid. Return cheesecloth bag with curd to the colander until whey is no longer dripping, about 1½ to 2 hours. If you like, add salt to taste. For creamy cottage cheese, stir in ⅓ cup rich milk or cream.

Garlic Almonds

Makes 1 pound

- 1 tablespoon unsalted butter
- 2 tablespoons soy sauce
- 2 teaspoons hot pepper sauce
- 3 garlic cloves, mashed
- 1 pound blanched whole almonds
- 3 teaspoons seasoned pepper
- ¼ teaspoon dried red pepper flakes
  Salt

Preheat oven to 350°F. Coat rimmed baking sheet with 1 tablespoon butter. Sprinkle with soy sauce, hot pepper sauce and garlic. Scatter almonds over sheet and stir with fork until well coated. Sprinkle with 1½ teaspoons seasoned pepper, dried pepper flakes and salt. Bake 10 minutes. Sprinkle almonds with remaining seasoned pepper and additional salt if desired. Stir with fork. Bake 15 minutes. Cool before serving.

Garlic Almonds can be stored in jar for up to 3 months.

Soy Nuts

Makes about 6 cups

    3 cups dried soybeans
    5 cups water

    ½ cup oil
      Salt

Soak soybeans overnight in water (check and add more water if necessary). Bring to boil and simmer 15 minutes, just to soften; skim off foam and hulls that float to surface. Drain well. Spread soybeans on flat surface and dry thoroughly.

Heat ¼ cup oil in large skillet. Add half the beans and sauté until golden brown, stirring frequently. Repeat with remaining soybeans and oil. Season lightly with salt.

Toasted Pumpkin Seeds

These are good when served as snacks or with cocktails.

Makes about 1 cup

- 2 cups unshelled pumpkin seeds, fibers rubbed off (not washed)
- 1 tablespoon peanut oil
- 1 tablespoon butter
- 1½ teaspoons coarse salt

Preheat oven to 250°F. Combine all ingredients in small bowl and mix well. Spead on baking sheet or in shallow pan and toast, stirring frequently, about 30 to 40 minutes, or until seeds are evenly browned and crisp. Cool, then store in tightly covered containers. Remove shells before eating.

2

Pickles, Chutneys and Relishes

Five-Day Pickles

Makes about ½ gallon

- 2 to 3 unpeeled, large cucumbers, thinly sliced
- 2 large onions, thinly sliced
- 2 cups sugar
- 2 cups white wine vinegar
- ¾ teaspoon celery seed
- ¾ teaspoon lemon pepper
- ¾ teaspoon turmeric
- ¾ teaspoon mustard seed
- ¼ teaspoon salt

Layer cucumber and onion in sterilized jars, packing tightly. Combine remaining ingredients in medium saucepan over low heat and stir constantly until sugar is dissolved, about 10 minutes. Pour evenly into jars and seal. Let cool slightly. Refrigerate at least 5 days before serving.

Japanese Sweet Pickle Slices

Makes 4 to 5 pints

- 4 pounds firm young cucumbers
- 6 cups distilled white vinegar
- 3½ cups sugar
- 3 tablespoons mustard seed
- 3 tablespoons coarse salt
- 1 tablespoon celery seed
- 1 tablespoon whole allspice
- 1 tablespoon pickling spice

Thinly slice unpeeled cucumbers (you will have approximately 4 quarts); set aside. Combine 4 cups vinegar, ½ cup sugar, mustard seed and salt in large kettle. Bring to boil over medium-high heat, stirring to dissolve sugar. Add cucumber slices. Return to boil for 15 minutes, stirring frequently. Transfer to colander and drain well, discarding cooking liquid. Let cool slightly.

Combine remaining vinegar and sugar with celery seed, allspice and pickling spice in same kettle. Bring to boil over medium-high heat, stirring to dissolve sugar. Pack cucumbers into sterilized jars. Pour hot liquid over cucumbers, covering completely. Seal and process in boiling water bath for 5 minutes.

Pickled Vegetables (Toursi)

During summer months, add green tomato wedges for a flavor twist.

Makes 8 pints

- 6 cups water
- 1 cup white wine vinegar
- ¾ cup olive oil
- 2 tablespoons salt
- 1 tablespoon garlic cloves, halved

4 cups diagonally sliced
celery (cut ½ inch thick)

3 cups cauliflower florets
(about 1 small head)

2 cups fresh string beans
(ends trimmed), cut in
half

2 cups sliced carrot (cut ½
inch thick)

8 fresh dill sprigs

8 fresh parsley sprigs

2 cups 1-inch green or red
bell pepper squares

6 red banana peppers,
seeded and cut into ½-
inch slices

6 yellow banana peppers,
seeded and cut into ½-
inch slices

1 8-ounce jar tiny cocktail
onions, drained

2 small zucchini, cut into
¼-inch slices (about 1
cup)

Feta cheese cut into
small cubes
Greek olives, tomato
wedges and cucumber
slices (optional)

Sterilize eight 1-pint jars. Combine water, vinegar, oil, salt and
garlic cloves in 5-quart Dutch

oven and bring to boil over medium-high heat. Add celery, cauliflower, beans, carrot, dill and parsley. Return to rapid boil and cook 3 minutes. Stir in green pepper, banana peppers, onions and zucchini and return to rapid boil. Remove from heat. Divide vegetables evenly among prepared jars using slotted spoon. Pour hot brine over vegetables to within ½ inch of top. Run long thin spatula or knife between inside of jar and vegetables to release any trapped air. Carefully wipe top of jar with towel. Cover tightly with lids. Refrigerate overnight before serving. *(Can be refrigerated up to 2 months.)*

To serve, arrange pickled vegetables in center of large platter. Surround with feta cheese cubes, Greek olives, tomato wedges and cucumber slices.

Recipe can be halved.

Pickled Vegetables with Oranges

Makes 1 quart

- ½ pound green beans (trimmed), halved crosswise
- ¼ pound snow peas, ends trimmed and strings removed

- 1¼ cups rice vinegar
- 1¼ cups water
- ½ cup sugar
- 2 dried red chilies, seeded
- 1 1-inch piece fresh ginger, very thinly sliced
- ½ teaspoon salt
- ¼ pound small oranges, very thinly sliced and seeded

Bring large amount of salted water to rapid boil over high heat. Add beans and cook until crisp-tender, about 5 to 6 minutes. Remove with slotted spoon and drain well. Rinse in cold water and drain again. Repeat with snow peas. Pat beans and snow peas dry.

Combine vinegar, water, sugar, chilies, ginger and salt in large saucepan over low heat and cook until sugar dissolves, swirling mixture occasionally. Increase heat and bring to boil. Let boil 5 minutes. Remove from heat and add orange slices. Let marinate until completely cool.

Pack beans, peas, ginger and orange slices evenly into 1-quart jar with tight-fitting lid. Pour in marinade. Refrigerate for at least 1 day or up to 3 days.

Dilled Brussels Sprouts

Makes 2 to 2½ quarts

 1½ pounds fresh brussels sprouts or 2 10-ounce packages frozen

 2 cups cider vinegar
 1 cup water
 ¾ cup sugar
 ¼ cup salt
 2 garlic cloves, minced
 1 large onion, thinly sliced
 4 to 5 sprigs fresh dill

Remove any brown or wilted outer leaves from brussels sprouts and trim stems. Wash well, place in steamer and steam until barely tender, about 8 to 10 minutes. *Do not overcook.*

Meanwhile, combine vinegar, water, sugar, salt and garlic in medium saucepan and bring to boil, stirring until sugar is dissolved. Layer sprouts and onion in sterilized pint jars. Tuck in 1 sprig dill for each jar. Pour hot vinegar mixture over and seal according to manufacturer's directions, or refrigerate. Let stand a few days before serving.

Pickled Cherries

Excellent served with pâté. Use as you would cornichons.

Makes about 4 quarts

   5 pounds fresh cherries, stems removed
   1 pound sugar
   2 quarts good quality red wine vinegar
   4 cinnamon sticks

Pack cherries in sterilized jars. Combine sugar, vinegar and cinnamon in 3-quart saucepan and bring to boil over medium-high heat, stirring frequently. Cook 5 minutes. Place cinnamon stick in each jar, pour hot syrup over and seal.

Cherries may be stored in jar in refrigerator for one year.

Apple Relish (Apfelkren)

This spicy Austrian relish is good with pork or goose.

Makes about 1½ cups

- 3 eating apples, peeled, cored and grated
- ¼ cup sugar or to taste
- 1 tablespoon prepared horseradish, drained
- 2 teaspoons paprika
- 2 tablespoons dry white wine (or more)

Combine all ingredients in medium bowl and blend well.

Quick Old-Fashioned Corn Relish

Makes about 1⅔ cups

- ½ cup vinegar
- ⅓ cup sugar
- 1 teaspoon salt
- ½ teaspoon celery seed
- ¼ teaspoon mustard seed
- ¼ teaspoon hot pepper sauce

- 1½ cups cooked corn kernels or 16-ounce can whole kernel corn, drained
- 2 tablespoons chopped green bell pepper
- 1 tablespoon chopped pimiento
- 1 tablespoon minced white or green onion

Combine first 6 ingredients in medium saucepan and bring to boil. Cook 2 minutes; remove from heat and cool.

Place remaining ingredients in medium bowl. Add cooled mixture and blend lightly. Chill.

This will keep indefinitely in the refrigerator; the flavor improves with standing.

Apple Chutney

A delicious complement to curries, pork and poultry.

Makes about 7½ pints

    8 cups peeled and
      chopped tart apples
 4½ cups sugar
    2 cups seedless golden
      raisins
    1 cup coarsely chopped
      toasted pecans or
      walnuts
  ½ cup vinegar
      Peel of 2 oranges, finely
      chopped
  ⅓ teaspoon cloves

Combine all ingredients in large kettle or Dutch oven. Place over high heat and bring to rolling boil, stirring constantly. Reduce heat to simmer and cook slowly until apples are tender and syrup is very thick and almost caramelized. Ladle into hot sterilized jars, seal and store in cool, dark, dry place. Keep refrigerated after opening.

Chutney may also be frozen.

Tomato-Apple Chutney

This spicy mixture is excellent with curries or roasted meats and makes a great gift.

Makes 1½ gallons

- 12 large ripe tomatoes, finely chopped
- 12 large green apples, finely chopped
- 8 medium onions, finely chopped
- 2 large green bell peppers, seeded and finely chopped
- 1½ quarts white vinegar
- 4 cups light brown sugar
- 2 cups golden raisins
- 4 teaspoons salt
- ⅓ cup mixed pickling spices, tied in cheesecloth bag

Combine all ingredients in large pot and bring to boil. Reduce heat to simmer and cook about 1½ hours, stirring frequently, until mixture is thick and syrupy. Remove spice bag.

Ladle into boiling hot sterilized pint jars and seal according to manufacturer's directions. Cool. Store in cool, dry place.

Chutney may also be stored in refrigerator or frozen.

Pear Chutney

Makes about 1½ to 2 quarts

  4 pounds pears, peeled, cored and chopped
2½ cups light brown sugar
  2 cups white vinegar
1½ cups golden raisins
 ½ cup chopped onion
 ½ cup chopped crystallized ginger
  2 tablespoons mustard seed, crushed in mortar or blender
  1 tablespoon salt
  3 garlic cloves, minced
 ½ teaspoon ground red pepper

Combine all ingredients in large saucepan and bring to boil over medium heat, stirring frequently. Reduce heat to simmer and cook until thick, about 40 to 50 minutes, stirring occasionally. Pour into hot, sterilized pint jars and seal according to manufacturer's directions.

3

Meat, Fish and Pâté

Pickled Pork

6 to 8 servings

    2 pounds pork loin
       Pinch of brown
       peppercorn
 1½ teaspoons salt
    1 teaspoon saltpeter

Season pork with peppercorn, salt and saltpeter. Let stand in refrigerator 1 day. Steam in wok 1½ hours. Cool to room temperature. Trim fat, slice thinly.

Carolina Pickled Shrimp

6 to 8 servings

- ½ cup vegetable oil
- ⅓ cup catsup
- ⅓ cup white vinegar
- 2 tablespoons Worcestershire sauce
- 2 teaspoons sugar
- 1 teaspoon salt
- ½ teaspoon dry mustard
  Dash of hot pepper sauce
- 1 pound cooked shelled shrimp
- 2 small red onions, thinly sliced
- 2 bay leaves, crushed

Combine first 8 ingredients and blend well. Layer shrimp, onion and bay leaves in bowl. Pour dressing over. Cover and chill before serving.

Almond Pâté

Serve with crackers or crudités.

Makes about 2½ cups

- 1 8-ounce package ripe Brie, rind discarded, then brought to room temperature
- ¾ cup (1½ sticks) butter, room temperature
- ½ cup toasted slivered almonds
- 2 tablespoons dry Sherry
- ¼ teaspoon dried thyme

Whip all ingredients together. Spoon into cheese crock; cover and chill at least 2 hours. Let stand at room temperature for about 1 hour before serving.

JEANNE

Mushroom and Nut Pâté

6 servings

- 2 tablespoons (¼ stick) butter
- 1 pound mushrooms, sliced
- 1 small onion, sliced
- 1 garlic clove, minced

- ¾ cup toasted slivered almonds
- ¼ cup toasted hazelnuts
- 2 tablespoons peanut oil
- ¼ teaspoon dried thyme
  Salt
  Dash of ground red pepper

  Toasted sesame seeds (garnish)

  Assorted crackers

Melt butter in large skillet over medium-high heat. Add mushrooms, onion and garlic and sauté until most of liquid has evaporated. Remove from heat.

Coarsely chop almonds and hazelnuts in blender or processor; remove 2 tablespoons and set aside. Continue chopping, slowly adding oil until mixture is well blended. Add seasoning and mushroom mixture and blend thoroughly. Stir in remaining nuts. Mold into loaf and sprinkle with sesame seeds. Serve with assorted crackers.

Pâté Maison

Makes 1 9 × 5-inch loaf

- 2 quarts water
- 2 teaspoons peppercorns
- 2 teaspoons whole cloves
- 3 bay leaves
  Few sprigs parsley

- 2½ pounds very fresh chicken livers

- 2 cups (4 sticks) butter, softened
- 1 small onion, finely chopped
- 1 large garlic clove, minced
- 1 tablespoon salt
- 2 teaspoons dry mustard
- ½ teaspoon freshly grated nutmeg
  Dash of hot pepper sauce
- ¼ cup brandy

Combine first 5 ingredients in a 4-quart saucepan. Bring to a boil and simmer 10 minutes. Strain.

Add chicken livers to liquid. Cook just below simmering point until liquid is clear and rosy and livers are done, about 10 minutes. Drain and pass through meat grinder. Set aside.

In a large mixing bowl, blend together remaining ingredients except brandy. Add liver and mix until smooth. Stir in brandy.

Line a 9 × 5-inch loaf pan with aluminum foil. Pack pâté into pan. Chill thoroughly before serving. *Flavors will develop more fully if pâté is allowed to chill overnight.*

JEANNE

Rillettes de New York

Makes about 2½ quarts

- 2 pounds pork leaf lard, back fat or lard
- 4 pounds pork shoulder, cut into 2-inch cubes
- 1 cup water

- 2 teaspoons salt
- ½ teaspoon freshly ground white pepper
- ¼ teaspoon allspice
- ⅛ teaspoon cinnamon

Melt fat in heavy deep skillet over medium-high heat. Add meat and water. Reduce heat to as low as possible and simmer gently until very tender, about 4 to 6 hours; do not boil. (*Can also be cooked in 250°F oven.*)

Pour off fat and reserve. Transfer meat to large bowl and shred using 2 forks. Mix in salt, pepper, allspice and cinnamon. Gradually mash in enough reserved fat to form paste (about 3 cups total; this may take 10 to 15 minutes). Pack mixture into small ramekins, crocks or jars. Strain remaining fat through several layers of moistened cheesecloth and pour over rillettes thinly to form airtight seal. Cover with parchment paper or aluminum foil. Store in refrigerator for up to 2 weeks. Serve at room temperature.

For variation, add 4 unpeeled garlic cloves to meat while cooking. Remove garlic before shredding the cooked meat.

4

Sauces, Dressings and Dips

Sauce Andalouse

This mayonnaise-based sauce is a marvelous accompaniment to cold chicken or poached salmon. Try it, too, with hard-cooked eggs or in egg, potato, seafood or chicken salads.

Makes about 2½ cups

- 2 large beefsteak tomatoes or 4 medium tomatoes
- ½ red bell pepper, seeded, or 4 ounces canned pimientos, drained
- 1 teaspoon olive oil

> 1 teaspoon tarragon or
>   chives, or combination
> 2 cups mayonnaise

Peel, seed and mince tomatoes with red pepper or pimientos. Place in medium skillet with oil and sauté over *lowest heat* (use a flame tamer, if available) approximately 1½ hours, stirring occasionally, until tomato mixture has reduced to a paste and cooked down to about ¾ cup.

Remove from heat and add herbs. Cool, then fold into mayonnaise, mixing to blend well.

This sauce may be refrigerated for as long as 2 weeks.

Tomato Meat Sauce

San Rufillo, a small trattoria in Italy, is famous for this marvelous sauce. It's wonderful on spaghetti, eggplant Parmesan or in any recipe calling for a red Italian meat sauce.

Makes ½ gallon

> 2 tablespoons olive oil
> 1 cup diced onion
> 2 garlic cloves, minced

1½ cups grated carrot
1 pound lean ground beef

1 28-ounce can tomato puree or Italian plum tomatoes
1 8-ounce jar marinara sauce
1 6-ounce can tomato paste
½ pound mushrooms, thinly sliced
½ cup diced green bell pepper
1 tablespoon chopped fresh parsley
1 teaspoon salt
1 teaspoon dried oregano
1 teaspoon dried basil
1 bay leaf
½ teaspoon white pepper
½ teaspoon allspice
⅛ teaspoon crushed red pepper
½ cup dry red wine

Heat oil in 4- to 5-quart saucepan over medium-high heat. Add onion and garlic and sauté, stirring constantly, until lightly browned. Reduce heat to medium, add carrot and cook, stirring, until softened. Add meat and cook, stirring, until crumbly and all liquid has evaporated.

Reduce heat to low. Add all remaining ingredients except wine and simmer uncovered 1½ hours, stirring occasionally. Blend in wine and simmer ½ hour more. Adjust seasonings.

Sauce may be refrigerated up to 5 days or frozen up to 4 months.

Green Goddess Dressing and Dipping Sauce

Makes about 2½ cups

> 1¼ cups homemade mayonnaise
>
> 1 cup sour cream
>
> ½ cup coarsely chopped fresh parsley
>
> ⅓ cup coarsely chopped green onion
>
> 1 2-ounce can anchovies, drained and rinsed
>
> 1 tablespoon fresh lemon juice
>
> 3 to 4 tablespoons wine vinegar

Generous pinch of
tarragon
Generous pinch of
chervil
Salt and freshly ground
pepper

Combine all ingredients in
blender or food processor and
blend until smooth. Refrigerate
overnight before serving.

Will keep 4 days in refrigerator.

Chinese Dipping Sauces

These 3 sauces may be used
with egg rolls, fried shrimp,
meats or fish. All of the following can be doubled or tripled.

Chinese Mustard Sauce

¼ cup boiling water
¼ cup dry mustard
2 teaspoons vegetable oil
½ teaspoon salt

Add water to mustard and mix
to blend well. Stir in oil and salt.

Chinese Red Sauce

3 tablespoons catsup
3 tablespoons chili sauce

1 to 2 tablespoons
prepared horseradish
(not cream style)
1 teaspoon fresh lemon
juice
Dash of hot pepper
sauce

Combine all ingredients in small
bowl and mix well.

Chinese Plum Sauce

1 cup plum preserves
⅓ cup dry Sherry
½ teaspoon ground cloves
½ teaspoon ground anise
½ teaspoon ground fennel
½ cup dry mustard (about
1 small can) or to taste

Combine all ingredients except
mustard in blender or food processor. Add mustard a little at a
time, blending well and adding
more mustard, until sauce is as
hot and spicy as desired (longer
blending makes a hotter sauce).

Flavored Vinegars

Inspired by a piquant combination of herbs and spices, a collection of flavored vinegars lets the cook create unique salad dressings and add zest to any number of dishes.

To add the flavoring, start with commercial distilled white, cider, red or white wine vinegar placed in a crock or large container. Add fresh herbs and/or spices and let stand for several weeks. Strain into clean bottles, adding the herbs if desired, and cap tightly.

A shorter version calls for bringing the combined ingredients to a boil and simmering for a few minutes. Cool, strain into clean bottles and seal.

Bottles with unusual shapes make attractive decanters for these vinegar creations.

To 1 quart vinegar add any of the following ingredients:

- 4 ounces fresh herbs,
  such as tarragon, thyme,
  sage, marjoram, dill or
  mint
- 24 red chili peppers
- Several garlic cloves,
  peeled and minced
  1 tablespoon salt
- 1 cup fresh rose petals
- 3 horseradish roots,
  freshly grated
  ¼ teaspoon ground red
  pepper
  ½ teaspoon *each* freshly
  ground black pepper
  and celery seed
- 1 cup finely chopped
  onion or 4 ounces sliced
  shallot
- 2 cinnamon sticks
  4 blades mace or 1
  tablespoon ground mace
  8 peppercorns
  12 cloves
  15 whole allspice

5

Crackers and Breads

Cheese Crackers

Makes about 2 dozen

- 1 cup all purpose flour
- ¼ teaspoon salt
- 6 tablespoons (¾ stick) butter
- 1 cup crisp rice cereal
- 1 cup grated sharp cheddar cheese

- 1 egg
- ½ teaspoon hot pepper sauce

Combine flour and salt in large bowl. Cut in butter until mixture resembles coarse meal. Add cereal and cheese, stirring with fork until thoroughly mixed.

Beat egg with hot pepper sauce in small bowl. Drizzle evenly over cheese mixture and blend well. Transfer dough to large piece of foil. Divide dough in half and form into 2 cylinders, each about 1½ inches thick. Cover and chill at least 15 minutes.

Preheat oven to 350°F. Cut cylinders into ¼-inch slices. Arrange on baking sheet and press lightly with fingertips. Bake until golden and crisp, about 20 to 25 minutes. Let cool. *Store in airtight container.*

Rye Salt Flutes

Makes 8 flutes

- 3 cups buttermilk
- 2 tablespoons dehydrated minced onion
- 2 tablespoons caraway seed
- 2 tablespoons whole dill seed
- 2 tablespoons oil
- 2 tablespoons salt
- 9⅔ cups unbleached all purpose flour

    1 pint cottage cheese,
       room temperature
    4 envelopes dry yeast
2⅓ cups rye flour

    1 egg white
       Coarse salt
    8 teaspoons caraway seed

Lightly grease large bowl and
baking sheet or bread flute baking pans; set aside.

Combine first 6 ingredients in 2-
quart saucepan. Place over medium heat and warm to 120°F,
stirring frequently. Transfer to
mixing bowl and add 4½ cups
white flour, cottage cheese and
yeast. Beat until thoroughly
blended, about 2 to 3 minutes.
Add rye flour, blending in well.
Beat in enough additional white
flour, ½ cup at a time, to make
a soft dough.

Turn out onto lightly floured
board and knead until smooth
and elastic. Place dough in
greased bowl, cover with plastic
wrap and hot damp towel and
let rise in warm place until double in volume. Punch dough
down and divide into 8 rolls,
each about 1¼ inches in diam-

eter. Place on prepared baking sheet or in pans, cover with plastic wrap and let rise until doubled in size.

Preheat oven to 350°F. Beat egg white lightly and brush over flutes. Sprinkle each with a little salt and 1 teaspoon caraway seed. Bake until crust is golden brown and bread sounds hollow when tapped, about 20 minutes. Remove from pans and cool on racks.

Lavash

This Middle Eastern sesame cracker bread keeps for months wrapped in plastic or foil. Store in a dry place.

Makes 12 to 15 crackers

  1¼ pounds (about 5 cups)
       unbleached all purpose
       flour
    1 envelope dry yeast
  2¼ teaspoons salt
   ¾ teaspoon sugar
   ¼ cup (½ stick) butter,
       melted

1¼ to 1½ cups warm water
(120°F to 130°F)

¾ to 1 cup sesame seeds

Grease or butter a large bowl;
set aside.

Combine first 4 ingredients in
mixing bowl. Blend butter with
1 cup water and add gradually
to dry ingredients, beating con-
tinuously. If dough seems dry
add more water as needed. Beat
or knead until dough is smooth
and elastic. Place in greased
bowl, turning to coat entire surface. Cover with plastic wrap
and hot damp towel and let rise
in warm place until doubled in
bulk, about 1 to 2 hours.

Remove oven racks from gas
oven; with electric oven place
bottom rack in lowest position
and place baking sheet on rack.
Preheat gas oven to 350°F, electric oven to 375°F. Divide dough
into pieces about the size of ten-
nis balls. Spread sesame seeds
on large breadboard or counter
top. Working with one piece of
dough at a time (keep remaining
dough covered), place on board

and *roll out as thinly as possible* without tearing dough.

Bake lavash, one at a time, until light golden with darker highlights, about 2 to 3 minutes on floor of gas oven or about 13 minutes in electric oven. Cool on racks.

Oatcakes

Makes 4 to 5 dozen 3-inch squares

   6 cups rolled oats
   3 cups unsifted all purpose flour
   1 cup sugar
   1 teaspoon salt
   ½ teaspoon baking soda
   2 cups vegetable shortening
   5 tablespoons cold water

   Whole wheat or graham flour

Mix oats, flour, sugar, salt and soda together until evenly blended. Cut in shortening until mixture resembles coarse meal. Add cold water 1 tablespoon at a time, blending after each addition, until mixture forms a ball.

Preheat oven to 375°F. Flour a board with whole wheat or graham flour and form dough into two balls. Roll each into a rectangle approximately ¼ inch thick. Cut into 3-inch squares and bake 15 to 20 minutes, or until slightly browned on top.

Oatcakes are best baked a day before serving. Store in an airtight container.

Deli Corn Rye

This tastes just like the bread used by your favorite deli for marvelous mile-high corned beef sandwiches.

Makes 1 loaf or 2 rounds

- 6 tablespoons yellow cornmeal
- ½ cup cold water
- 1 cup boiling water
- 2 teaspoons salt
- 1 tablespoon butter

- 1 envelope dry yeast or 1 cake compressed yeast, crumbled

   2½ cups rye flour
   1½ cups sifted unbleached
        all purpose flour
    1   cup cold mashed
        potatoes
    1   tablespoon caraway seed

        Cornmeal

    ¼   cup water
    ½   teaspoon cornstarch

    1   teaspoon caraway seed

Lightly grease large bowl for rising and set aside.

Combine cornmeal and cold
water in 2-quart saucepan over
medium-high heat. Add boiling
water and cook 2 minutes, stirring constantly. Stir in salt and
butter. Let cool to lukewarm.

Combine yeast, rye and all purpose flour, potatoes and 1 tablespoon caraway seed in mixing
bowl and mix to blend. Add
cornmeal mixture and blend
thoroughly. Turn onto lightly
floured board and knead until
stiff but still slightly sticky. Place
in greased bowl, turning to coat
entire surface. Cover with plastic wrap and hot damp towel

and let rise in warm place until doubled in volume.

Grease baking sheet and sprinkle lightly with cornmeal. Punch dough down, shape into loaf or rounds and place on baking sheet. Cover with plastic wrap and let rise again until doubled in volume.

Preheat oven to 375°F. Bake bread 40 minutes. Combine water and cornstarch in small saucepan and bring to boil over high heat; boil 1 minute.

Remove bread from oven, brush lightly with glaze and sprinkle with remaining caraway seed. Return bread to oven for about 5 minutes, or until top is glazed and loaf sounds hollow when tapped. Cool on rack.

Flowerpot Cheese Bread

Makes 4 loaves

    4 red clay flowerpots, 5 inches wide by 5 inches deep with 4-inch base
       Vegetable shortening

1¾ cups water, 120° to 130°F
    3 tablespoons butter
    2 tablespoons honey
    4 large eggs
    1 egg white
    7 cups unbleached all purpose flour
    2 envelopes dry yeast
    1 tablespoon sugar
    2 teaspoons salt
    1 teaspoon baking powder
    2 cups shredded sharp or medium cheddar cheese

    1 egg yolk, beaten
       Poppy seed

Preheat oven to 375°F. Wash and generously grease flowerpots with shortening. Bake 5 to 10 minutes or until pots are heated and shortening has been absorbed. Regrease and bake 5 to 10 minutes more. Set aside to cool. When cool, butter pots generously and line sides with buttered waxed paper. Do not line bottom.

Lightly grease large bowl for rising and set aside.

Combine water, butter and honey in mixing bowl. Beat in 4 eggs and egg white, 3½ cups flour, yeast, sugar and salt, mixing until thoroughly combined. Continue to beat 2 minutes, then add baking powder and additional flour ½ cup at a time, beating constantly until soft dough is formed. Quickly mix in cheddar cheese.

Turn dough onto lightly floured board and knead until smooth and elastic, about 10 minutes (kneading will thoroughly mix in cheese). Place in prepared bowl, turning to coat entire surface. Cover with plastic wrap and hot damp towel and let stand in warm place until doubled in volume. Punch down and let rise again until doubled.

Punch dough down once more and turn out onto lightly floured board. Knead about 2 minutes, then divide into 4 equal sections. Knead briefly, then separate each section into 7 to 10 balls. Layer balls of dough in each pot, placing last ball in center. Repeat with remaining pots. Cover lightly with plastic wrap and allow dough to rise in a warm place to top of pots.

Preheat oven to 425°F. Brush each bread with egg yolk and sprinkle lightly with poppy seed. Place double thickness of foil on oven rack. Bake bread 10 minutes. Reduce heat to 375°F and bake until bread is golden brown and sounds hollow when tapped, about 25 to 30 minutes. If top browns too fast, cover with foil. Cool pots on rack 15 minutes, then carefully remove bread and let cool.

Fresh Apple Nut Bread

Makes 1 9 × 5-inch loaf

- ¼ cup (½ stick) butter, room temperature
- 1 cup firmly packed light brown sugar
- 2 eggs
- 3 cups unsifted flour
- 2 cups peeled grated apple (about 2 large)
- ¾ cup chopped nuts
- 1½ teaspoons baking soda
- 1 teaspoon baking powder
- 1 teaspoon grated lemon peel
- 1 teaspoon salt
- 1 teaspoon cinnamon
- ¼ teaspoon freshly grated nutmeg
- ¾ cup buttermilk

Preheat oven to 350°F. Grease and flour 9 × 5-inch loaf pan. Cream butter and sugar in medium bowl. Beat in eggs. Combine next 9 ingredients in separate bowl and blend into creamed mixture alternately with buttermilk. Turn into pan and bake until toothpick inserted in center comes out clean, about 1 hour. Cool 10 minutes. Remove from pan and cool completely on wire rack.

Banana Nut Bread

Makes 1 9 × 5-inch loaf or 2 5⅝ × 3⅛-inch loaves

- ½ cup (1 stick) butter, room temperature
- 1 cup sugar
- 2 eggs, beaten
- 2 tablespoons sour milk
- 1 teaspoon fresh lemon juice
- ½ teaspooon baking soda
- 1½ teaspoons baking powder
- ¼ teaspoon salt
- 4 large very ripe bananas, mashed
- 2 cups all purpose flour
- 1½ cups walnuts or pecans

Preheat oven to 350°F. Grease and flour 1 9 × 5-inch loaf pan or 2 smaller pans. Cream butter, sugar and eggs in large bowl using electric mixer. Add remaining ingredients and mix on low until blended. Turn into pan(s) and bake until toothpick inserted in center comes out clean, about 1 hour. Cool 10 minutes. Remove from pan and cool completely on wire rack.

Blueberry Quick Bread

Makes 1 bundt cake, 2 9 × 5-inch loaves or 4 5⅜ × 3⅛-inch loaves

5	cups all purpose flour
1½	cups sugar
2	tablespoons baking powder
1	teaspoon cinnamon
1	teaspoon salt
¾	cup (1½ sticks) butter
1½	cups chopped walnuts
1	teaspoon grated lemon peel
4	eggs
2	cups milk
2	teaspoons vanilla
	Juice of 1 lemon
3	cups fresh or frozen blueberries, unthawed

Preheat oven to 350°F. Grease and flour 10-inch bundt or smaller pans. Combine flour, sugar, baking powder, cinnamon and salt in large bowl. Cut in butter until mixture resembles fine crumbs. Stir in walnuts and lemon peel.

Beat eggs lightly with fork in small bowl. Stir in milk, vanilla and lemon juice and mix well. Blend into flour mixture just until moistened. Gently stir in blueberries. Spoon evenly into pan(s) and bake until toothpick inserted in center comes out clean, about 80 to 90 minutes. Cool on wire rack 10 minutes. Remove from pan. Serve warm or cold. Wrap and refrigerate.

Cranberry Nut Bread

Makes 1 9 × 5-inch loaf

   2 cups sifted all purpose flour
   1 cup sugar
1½ teaspoons baking powder
   1 teaspoon salt
  ½ teaspoon baking soda
  ¼ cup vegetable shortening
   1 egg, well beaten
  ¾ cup orange juice
   1 teaspoon grated orange peel

1 cup fresh cranberries,
  coarsely chopped, or 1
  cup well-drained canned
  whole cranberries,
  coarsely chopped
½ cup chopped walnuts or
  pecans

Preheat oven to 350°F. Grease and flour 9 × 5-inch loaf pan. Sift dry ingredients into large bowl. Cut in shortening. Combine egg, orange juice and peel and add to dry ingredients, mixing just to moisten. Fold in berries and nuts. Turn into pan and bake until toothpick inserted in center comes out clean, about 1 hour. Cool on wire rack before removing from pan. Wrap and store overnight.

Pineapple-Zucchini Loaf

Makes 2 9 × 5-inch loaves

3 eggs
2 cups sugar
1 cup oil
3 tablespoons vanilla
2 cups peeled, grated and
  well-drained zucchini

   3 cups all purpose flour
   1 teaspoon baking powder
   1 teaspoon baking soda
   1 teaspoon salt
   1 8-ounce can crushed
     pineapple, undrained
   1 cup chopped pecans or
     walnuts
  ½ cup raisins (optional)

Preheat oven to 350°F. Grease and flour 2 9 × 5-inch loaf pans. Beat eggs until fluffy. Add sugar, oil and vanilla and blend well. Add zucchini. Sift together flour, baking powder, soda and salt and add to batter. Stir in pineapple, nuts and raisins, if desired, and mix well. Turn into pans and bake until toothpick inserted in center comes out clean, about 1 hour. Cool on wire rack before removing from pans. Wrap and store overnight to develop flavors before slicing.

Joan's Pumpkin Bread

Makes 4 1-pound loaves

   4 cups sugar
   1 29-ounce can pumpkin
   3 eggs

1 cup oil
5 cups all purpose flour
1 tablespoon baking soda
2 teaspoons cinnamon
1½ teaspoons ground cloves
1 teaspoon salt
2 cups coarsely chopped dates
2 cups coarsely chopped toasted walnuts

Whipped cream cheese (optional)

Preheat oven to 350°F. Grease 4 1-pound coffee cans or 8 × 4-inch loaf pans.

Combine sugar, pumpkin and eggs in large bowl and beat by hand or with mixer until well blended. Add oil and beat to combine. Thoroughly blend in flour, soda, cinnamon, cloves and salt. Stir in dates and nuts. Fill prepared pans ¾ full to allow for rising during baking. Bake about 1 hour or until toothpick inserted near center of loaf comes out clean and bread has pulled away slightly from sides of pan. Serve with whipped cream cheese.

Bread may be baked in ring molds, cupcake pans or other small pans; test after 20 minutes for doneness.

Bread may be frozen indefinitely.

Russian Kulich

This rich yeast coffee cake, fragrant with almonds, fruits, a touch of rum and saffron, was served in old Russia accompanied by rich, creamy Paskha (see recipe page 84).

Makes 1 large or 2 medium loaves

- ½ teaspoon saffron
- ¼ cup dark rum
- ½ cup sliced glacéed fruits (cherries, angelica, pineapple, citron)
- ½ cup raisins
- 1 cup sliced almonds, toasted and coarsely chopped
- 1 cup sifted all purpose flour

3 tablespoons yeast
¼ cup milk, scalded and
  cooled to lukewarm
2 tablespoons light brown
  sugar

¾ cup (1½ sticks) unsalted
  butter
1 cup light brown sugar
1 teaspoon anise extract
1 teaspoon almond extract
3 egg yolks
1 cup whipping cream,
  warmed slightly
4 to 5 cups all purpose
  flour

3 egg whites

Egg White Frosting
1 beaten egg white
2 cups powdered sugar
1 teaspoon vanilla or
  almond extract or 2
  teaspoons lemon juice

Slivered almonds
Colored sprinkles
(garnish)
Paskha (optional, see
recipe page 84)

Soak saffron in rum an hour or more. Combine fruits, raisins and almonds with 1 cup flour. Set aside.

Dissolve yeast with milk and 2 tablespoons brown sugar. Allow to stand until frothy, about 5 to 10 minutes.

In electric mixer, cream butter and sugar until smooth. Add extracts, yolks and warm cream. Beat in yeast mixture thoroughly. Add 4 cups flour and beat until smooth and elastic, adding additional flour as necessary. Place in an oiled bowl, turning to coat top of dough. Cover with plastic wrap and a towel wrung out in hot water. Allow to rise in warm place until doubled in size.

Punch dough down. Turn out onto lightly floured board and knead in floured fruits and nuts, saffron and rum. (If the addition of the fruit-nut mixture and rum moistens the dough to the point of stickiness, add additional flour ¼ cup at a time. Dough should be on the soft side, just firm enough to cut without sticking, so add no more flour than necessary.)

Beat egg whites until stiff. Fold into dough. (A metal scraper or spatula will help incorporate whites completely. Sprinkle with a bit more flour to cut any stickiness.)

Thoroughly oil two 2-pound coffee cans. Cut and oil waxed paper circles to fit bottom of cans. Fill each can halfway with dough. Moisten fingers and pat tops smooth. Cover with waxed paper and allow to rise in a warm place until dough reaches no higher than top edge of cans.

Bake at 375°F for 20 minutes; turn heat down to 325°F and bake 40 minutes. (If bread is browning too fast, reduce heat to 300°F.) Test with a metal skewer inserted in center of bread. If moist particles cling to skewer, return bread to oven for 10 more minutes.

Allow bread to cool 10 minutes before turning out of cans, using a long thin knife to loosen.

For frosting, beat egg white until
stiff. Slowly beat in sugar and
flavoring. Frost top of bread
while still warm, allowing frosting to run down the sides. Top
with slivered almonds or colored sprinkles. To serve, cut
slices horizontally, reserving the
decorated top slice as a lid to
prevent cut edge from drying.
Serve with Paskha.

Hot Cross Buns

These golden brown buns
loaded with spices and currants are topped with a powdered sugar icing.

Makes about 1½ dozen

4	to 5 cups all purpose flour
⅓	cup sugar
½	teaspoon salt
1¼	teaspoons cinnamon
½	teaspoon freshly grated nutmeg
¼	teaspoon cloves
1	tablespoon yeast
1	cup milk
¼	cup (½ stick) butter

2 eggs, room temperature

1 cup currants or raisins
1 tablespoon finely grated
   lemon peel

1 egg yolk beaten with 2
   tablespoons water

Frosting
1 cup powdered sugar
1 teaspoon fresh lemon
   juice
1 tablespoon hot milk
½ teaspoon vanilla

In large bowl thoroughly mix 1½
cups flour, sugar, salt, spices and
yeast. Heat milk and butter in
saucepan over low heat until
warm (110°F). Gradually add to
dry ingredients and beat 2 minutes with electric mixer at medium speed, scraping sides of
bowl occasionally.

Add eggs and ½ cup flour (or
enough to make a thick batter).
Beat at high speed 2 minutes,
scraping bowl occasionally.
Gradually stir in 2 cups flour to
make a soft dough, adding any
additional flour 2 tablespoons at
a time if needed. Dough should
be soft, *not stiff*.

Turn dough out onto lightly floured surface, kneading until smooth and elastic, about 8 to 10 minutes (5 minutes with dough hook). Place in oiled bowl, turning to coat top of dough. Cover with plastic wrap and a towel wrung out in hot water. Allow to rise in warm place until doubled in bulk, about 1 hour.

Punch dough down and turn out onto lightly floured surface. Knead in currants or raisins and lemon peel. Divide into 18 equal pieces, forming each piece into a ball. Place in 2 well-oiled 9-inch round cake pans.

Brush buns with combined egg yolk and water. Cover with waxed paper and allow to rise in warm place until doubled in size, about 1 hour.

Preheat oven to 375°F. Cut a cross on top of each bun with knife or scissors. Bake 20 to 25 minutes, or until golden. Remove from pans and cool on wire racks. Combine all frosting ingredients, form cross atop buns.

6

Jams and Preserves

Peach Jam

Makes 3 cups

> 5 cups peeled, chopped ripe peaches (about 3 pounds)
>   Juice of 1 large lemon
> 3 cups sugar
> 2 teaspoons orange flower water

Prepare 3 half-pint jars. Combine peaches and lemon juice in Dutch oven or large kettle and simmer gently until peaches are soft. Add sugar and stir until dissolved. Increase heat to high and bring to hard boil. Let boil until setting point is reached, about 15 minutes. Stir in orange flower water and boil another minute. Skim foam from surface. Pour jam into sterilized jars to within ¼ inch from top and seal. Process 5 minutes in boiling water bath. Remove from water and let stand undisturbed until cooled. Test for seal by pressing down on center of lid; it should stay down. Store in cool dark place.

Chunky Apricot Preserves

This easy preserve makes delightful gifts.

Makes about 3½ cups

- 1 6-ounce package dried apricots
- 1 cup water
- 4 cups sugar
- 1 8¼-ounce can crushed pineapple in its own juice, undrained
- 1 10-ounce package frozen yellow squash, thawed and drained (optional)

Combine apricots and water in
medium saucepan and let stand
about 1 hour to plump. Place
over medium heat and cook until apricots are tender, about 10
minutes. Mash into coarse
chunks. Add sugar, pineapple
and squash, blending well. Continue cooking over low heat until thickened, stirring occasionally, about 15 minutes. Pour into
sterilized half-pint jars and seal.
Let cool. Store in refrigerator.

Pumpkin Conserve

Makes about 2½ pints

    3 cups cooked pumpkin
   2½ cups firmly packed
       brown sugar
   1½ cups dried apricots,
       coarsely chopped
   1½ cups raisins, coarsely
       chopped
    2 tablespoons finely
       chopped candied ginger
    1 tablespoon freshly grated
       lemon peel
    1 tablespoon fresh lemon
       juice or to taste

Combine all ingredients in 3-quart saucepan. Place over low heat and cook, stirring frequently, about 45 minutes, or until thick. Pour into hot, sterilized half-pint jars and seal according to manufacturer's directions. Store in cool, dark and dry place.

Conserve may also be refrigerated for up to 1 month or frozen for up to 6 months.

Rhubarb Conserve

Makes approximately 1 quart

> 4 cups diced rhubarb (about 4 large stalks)
> 2½ cups sugar
> 1 cup raisins
> ¼ cup orange juice
> 1 tablespoon fresh lemon juice
> 1 tablespoon grated orange peel
> 1 tablespoon grated lemon peel
> ½ cup chopped nuts

Combine all ingredients except nuts in a large saucepan. Bring to a boil over medium heat, then reduce heat and simmer 30 to 40 minutes, stirring occasionally, until mixture is thick. Skim off foam and discard. Remove from heat and stir in nuts. Pour into hot, sterilized pint jars and seal, or refrigerate.

Raw Applesauce

Makes about 1½ cups

- 3 apples, peeled, cored and diced
- ¼ cup apple cider or juice *or* orange or grapefruit juice
- ¼ cup light corn syrup

Place all ingredients in blender or processor and puree.

Danish Applesauce

A zesty accompaniment that is particularly pleasing with game or poultry.

Makes about 1 quart

4 cups cooked pureed
   apples (4 to 5 large)
¼ cup sugar or to taste
   Grated rind and strained
   juice of ½ orange
   Grated rind and strained
   juice of ½ lemon
   Sherry

Combine all ingredients except
Sherry in medium bowl and mix
to blend. Add enough Sherry to
give the sauce a soft consistency.

JEANNE

7

Sweets

Chocolate Macaroons

Makes 2 to 2½ dozen

- 1 15-ounce can sweetened condensed milk
- 2 ounces unsweetened chocolate
- 2 cups shredded coconut
- 1 cup coarsely chopped nuts, or ½ cup nuts and ½ cup plumped, drained golden raisins
- 1 tablespoon strongly brewed coffee
- 1 teaspoon vanilla
- ⅛ teaspoon salt

Preheat oven to 350°F. Oil baking sheet. Combine milk and chocolate in top of double boiler. Place over boiling water on high heat and stir constantly until mixture thickens, about 5 minutes. Add remaining ingredients and stir to blend. Drop by teaspoonfuls onto prepared sheet and bake about 10 minutes, or until bottoms are set (watch carefully since they can burn easily). *Do not overbake; macaroons should have a soft, chewy texture.* Transfer to waxed paper–lined rack or plate and cool completely.

Windmill Cookies

Makes about 2 dozen

>   8 ounces cream cheese, room temperature
>   ¾ cup (1½ sticks) unsalted butter, room temperature
>   1 egg yolk
>   1½ cups all purpose flour
>   1 tablespoon baking powder
>
>   ½ cup (about) strawberry jam or currant jelly
>
>   Powdered sugar

Beat cream cheese, butter and yolk in large bowl until smooth.

Blend in flour and baking powder to form stiff dough. Divide in half. Wrap in plastic and flatten into disc. Refrigerate 1 hour.

Preheat oven to 350°F. Roll out half of dough between 2 sheets of plastic wrap to thickness of ⅛ inch. Cut into 3-inch squares. Transfer to ungreased baking sheets. On each square, make cut from each corner almost to center. Fold every other corner to center and press to seal. Place about 1 teaspoon jam or jelly in center of windmill. Bake until light golden, about 14 to 16 minutes. Transfer to rack. Repeat with remaining dough. Let cookies cool completely.

Sift powdered sugar lightly over cooled cookies.

Brown Sugar Pecan Brownies

Makes about 3 dozen

2½ cups all purpose flour
1 pound light brown sugar
1 cup (2 sticks) unsalted butter, cut into ½-inch pieces

2 eggs, room temperature
1 teaspoon vanilla

1½ teaspoons baking powder
Pinch of salt
1 cup chopped pecans

Preheat oven to 350°F. Lightly butter 9 × 13-inch baking pan. Combine 1¼ cups flour with ⅓ cup brown sugar in medium bowl. Cut in ½ cup butter until mixture resembles coarse meal. Press into bottom of prepared pan. Bake 15 minutes (retain oven at 350°F).

Meanwhile, cook remaining brown sugar and ½ cup butter in medium saucepan over low heat until sugar dissolves. Beat eggs in large bowl of electric mixer until pale yellow and ribbon forms when beaters are lifted. Gradually beat in brown sugar mixture. Stir in vanilla, blending thoroughly.

Sift remaining 1¼ cups flour with baking powder and salt. Blend into brown sugar mixture. Stir in pecans. Spread mixture over baked crust. Bake 25 minutes. Cool in pan on rack. Cut into squares. Wrap brownies tightly in plastic. *Store in airtight container.*

Baked Fudge

8 to 10 servings

> 2 cups sugar
> 4 eggs, room temperature, beaten to blend
> ½ cup all purpose flour
> ½ cup unsweetened cocoa powder
> 1 cup (2 sticks) butter, melted
> 1 cup chopped pecans
> 2 teaspoons vanilla
>   Unsweetened whipped cream (garnish)

Preheat oven to 325°F. Beat sugar and egg until mixture forms slowly dissolving ribbon when beaters are lifted. Sift flour and cocoa into mixture and blend well. Stir in melted butter, nuts and vanilla; do not overmix. Spread batter evenly in 8 × 10-inch baking pan. Set into larger pan; add enough boiling water to larger pan to come halfway up sides. Bake until fudge is firm and knife inserted in center comes out moist but clean, about 1 hour. Let cool. Cut into squares. Serve with usweetened whipped cream.

Triple-Chocolate Fudge

Makes two 9 × 13-inch pans

- 4½ cups sugar
- 1 teaspoon salt
- ½ cup (1 stick) butter
- 1 13-ounce can evaporated milk

- 1 12-ounce bag semisweet chocolate chips
- 4 4-ounce bars German's Sweet chocolate, broken into 1-inch chunks

9 ounces milk chocolate,
   broken into 1-inch
   chunks
1½ 7-ounce jars
   marshmallow cream
2 teaspoons vanilla
4 cups coarsely chopped
   nuts, toasted

In 6-quart Dutch oven, combine sugar, salt, butter and milk. Bring to simmer, stirring constantly, over medium heat. *As soon as first bubble is seen*, boil mixture exactly 8 minutes. Remove from heat immediately.

Quickly stir in remaining ingredients. Blend thoroughly. Pour into two oiled 9 × 13-inch pans. Cover with foil and refrigerate until firm. Slice as desired. Bring to room temperature before serving for fullest flavor. *Store in refrigerator or freezer.*

JEANNE

Macadamia Nut Fudge

Makes about 128 1-inch
squares

  4½ cups (2 pounds) sugar
   ½ cup (1 stick) unsalted
      butter
   1 13-ounce can evaporated
      milk
   3 4-ounce bars sweet
      cooking chocolate (best
      quality)
   1 12-ounce package
      semisweet chocolate
      chips
   1 7-ounce jar
      marshmallow cream
   1 teaspoon salt
   2 teaspoons vanilla
   3 cups coarsely chopped
      unsalted raw macadamia
      nuts (chop by placing in
      a plastic bag and
      pounding with mallet or
      heavy rolling pin)

Line two 9-inch square pans
with waxed paper. Combine
sugar, butter and milk in heavy
2-quart saucepan and bring to
simmer over medium heat. *At
first sign of a bubble* simmer 5
minutes, stirring constantly. Re-

move from heat and add all ingredients except 1 cup nuts.

Spread into pans. Sprinkle with remaining nuts, pressing lightly into surface. Chill until firm. Cut into squares.

English Plum Pudding

10 to 12 servings

- ½ cup brandy (or more)
- ¼ pound beef suet, ground
- 2½ cups fresh fine breadcrumbs
- 1¼ cups firmly packed light brown sugar
- 1¼ cups golden raisins
- 1¼ cups dark raisins
- 1¼ cups currants
- ¾ cup glacéed cherries
- ¾ cup slivered almonds
- ½ cup glacéed lemon peel
- ½ cup glacéed orange peel
- ½ cup all purpose flour
- 2 eggs, beaten
- 1 small tart green apple, peeled, cored and grated
  Grated peel of 1 orange
- 3 tablespoons molasses
- 1 teaspoon allspice
- 1 teaspoon cinnamon

1 teaspoon baking soda
½ teaspoon ground cloves
½ teaspoon salt
¼ teaspoon freshly grated nutmeg

Holly sprig (garnish)
¼ cup brandy
Hard Sauce (see following recipe)

Butter 2-quart pudding mold. Add water to large steamer to within 1 inch of rack. Cover and bring to boil over medium-high heat (do not let boiling water touch rack). Meanwhile, combine ½ cup brandy with all remaining ingredients (except garnish and sauce) in large bowl and mix thoroughly. Turn mixture into prepared mold. Cover with foil and tie tightly with string. Reduce heat to medium low, carefully remove steamer cover and set mold on rack. Cover and steam 4 hours, adding water occasionally to steamer as necessary. Store at room temperature at least 3 months, adding drops of brandy to pudding about once a week to moisten.

To serve, resteam pudding in same manner 1 hour. Invert pudding onto rimmed serving dish. Heat remaining ¼ cup brandy in small saucepan. Pour over pudding and ignite. Garnish with holly sprig. Pass Hard Sauce separately.

Hard Sauce

Makes about 1 cup

- ½ cup (1 stick) unsalted butter, room temperature
- ½ cup powdered sugar
- ⅛ teaspoon freshly grated nutmeg
- 2 tablespoons dark rum or brandy
- 1 teaspoon vanilla

Cream butter in medium bowl. Beat in powdered sugar and nutmeg. Blend in rum and vanilla. Chill until firm.

Paskha

Makes about 2 quarts

    4 8-ounce packages cream cheese, room temperature

    1 cup (2 sticks) butter, room temperature

    3 egg yolks

    2 cups powdered sugar

    1 package unflavored gelatin softened in 2 tablespoons cold water

    2 teaspoons vanilla

    1 cup whipping cream

    2 tablespoons kirsch

    ¾ cup slivered almonds, toasted

    1 cup fresh, firm strawberries, washed and hulled

    1 2-quart clay flowerpot, about 6 inches across top, well washed and dried

    Gumdrops (optional garnish)

Place cheese and butter in mixer bowl and beat at low speed until well blended. Add yolks one at a time. Gradually beat in sugar.

Place gelatin over hot water to dissolve. Blend into cheese mixture. Add vanilla. Whip cream with kirsch. Add to cheese. Blend in nuts. Slice strawberries and carefully fold in.

Line pot with cheesecloth wrung out in cold water. Spoon cheese mixture into pot, filling to brim. Cover with clear plastic and refrigerate overnight.

To unmold, place dessert plate over pot, inverting quickly. Gently lift off pot, tugging at cheesecloth if necessary. Remove cheesecloth. Decorate with gumdrops.

May be prepared and stored in pot in refrigerator up to 5 days.

JEANNE

Christmas Fruitcakes

Makes 5 cakes

- 1 pound pitted dates
- 1 pound dried apricot halves
- ½ pound Brazil nuts
- ½ pound walnut halves
- ½ pound pecan halves
- 1 cup diced glacéed fruit
- 1 cup drained maraschino cherries
- 3 ounces glacéed apricots, halved
- 1½ cups all purpose flour
- 1 teaspoon baking powder
- 1½ cups sugar
- 6 eggs, room temperature
- 2 teaspoons vanilla
- 1 teaspoon salt

Glacéed cherries and nuts (garnish)

- 1¼ cups brandy

Preheat oven to 300°F. Cut circles of waxed paper to fit bottoms of five 2-cup soufflé dishes. Grease dishes well and fit with foil collars. Combine first 8 ingredients in large bowl. Sift flour and baking powder over top. Stir until mixture is well coated.

Combine sugar, eggs, vanilla and salt in medium bowl and beat until slightly foamy. Pour egg mixture over fruit and nuts and blend gently. Divide evenly among prepared dishes. Lightly press mixture down into dishes. Garnish tops with cherries and nuts. Bake until tester inserted in centers comes out clean, about 1¼ hours.

Remove from oven and immediately drizzle each cake with 2 tablespoons brandy. Let cool. Discard foil collars. Remove cakes from dishes. Wash and dry dishes. Replace cakes. Drizzle each cake with 2 tablespoons brandy. When competely cool, wrap each cake in plastic, tissue and ribbon.

Index

Credits

The following people contributed the recipes included in this book:

Liz Barclay
Sharon Cadwallader
Casa Vieja, Corales, New Mexico
Irena Chalmers
Cecilia Chiang
Claudia Feurey
Naomi French
Gerri Gilliland
Connie Glenn
Bert Greene
Inverary Inn, Baddeck, Nova Scotia,
    Canada
Diane Jubelier
Lynne Kasper
Sophie Kay
Peter Kump
Rita Leinwand
Abby Mandel
Berenice McLaughlin
Jinx Morgan
Joyce Resnik
Arno Schmidt
Sylvia Schur
Tail of the Trout, Rogers, Arkansas,
    Karen Bloomfield, owner
Doris Tobias